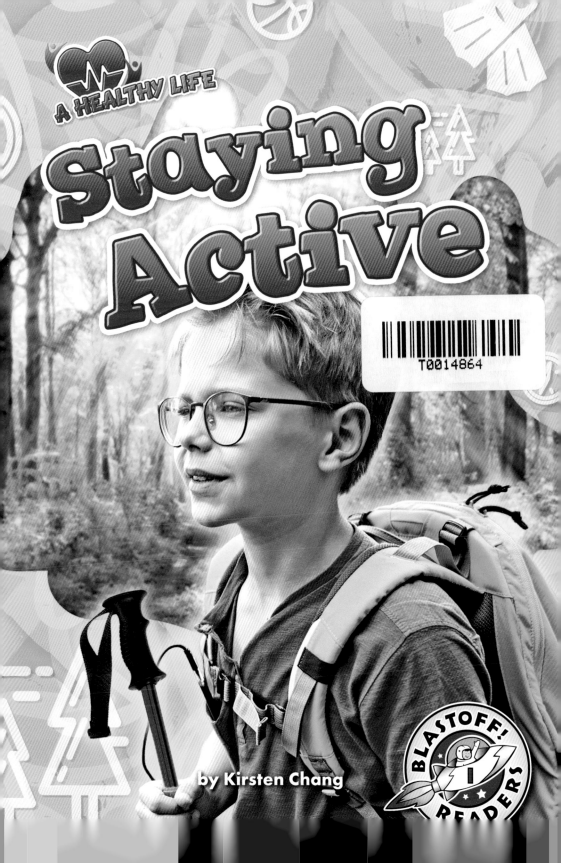

A HEALTHY LIFE

Staying Active

by Kirsten Chang

T0014864

BLASTOFF! READERS

Blastoff! Readers are carefully developed by literacy experts to build reading stamina and move students toward fluency by combining standards-based content with developmentally appropriate text.

Level 1 provides the most support through repetition of high-frequency words, light text, predictable sentence patterns, and strong visual support.

Level 2 offers early readers a bit more challenge through varied sentences, increased text load, and text-supportive special features.

Level 3 advances early-fluent readers toward fluency through increased text load, less reliance on photos, advancing concepts, longer sentences, and more complex special features.

★ **Blastoff! Universe**

Reading Level

Grade **K**

Grades **1–3**

Grade **4**

This edition first published in 2022 by Bellwether Media, Inc.

No part of this publication may be reproduced in whole or in part without written permission of the publisher. For information regarding permission, write to Bellwether Media, Inc., Attention: Permissions Department, 6012 Blue Circle Drive, Minnetonka, MN 55343.

Library of Congress Cataloging-in-Publication Data

LC record for Staying Active available at https://lccn.loc.gov/2021041252

Text copyright © 2022 by Bellwether Media, Inc. BLASTOFF! READERS and associated logos are trademarks and/or registered trademarks of Bellwether Media, Inc.

Editor: Rebecca Sabelko   Designer: Andrea Schneider

Printed in the United States of America, North Mankato, MN.

Table of Contents

Move Around

Troy likes to stay active. He hikes with his family. He plays soccer.

Why Is Staying Active Important?

Staying active is good for our bodies and our minds!

Our hearts, bones, and **muscles** work hard when we **exercise**. They become stronger.

Being active helps us
think clearly.
We learn better.

How Does Staying Active Help?

healthy body

learn better

sleep better

We often sleep better after exercise.
It is easier to **relax**.

Not being active
can raise our chances
of getting sick.

How Do We Stay Active?

It is important to exercise most days. Ella enjoys biking. Alex does **yoga**.

yoga

Cole takes breaks
from sitting.
He goes for a walk.